The Unplugged Vacation

How Accounting Firm Owners Can Take a Proper Holiday Without Checking Emails

Brannon Poe, CPA

The Unplugged Vacation

Independently Published

Copyright © 2021 Brannon Poe, CPA

Published in the United States of America

210216-01792.4

ISBN: 9798515042387

For more information on 90-Minute Books including finding out how you can publish your own book, visit 90minutebooks.com or call (863) 318-0464

Here's What's Inside…

Introduction

CPAs too often work insane hours, and many times, they still don't receive the financial rewards they deserve. We have been intermediaries that specialize in the sale of accounting firms since 2003. We've seen how smart owners have been able to build amazing firms that are highly profitable. One thing that we've observed over and over is that often in high-performing firms, the owners have developed great boundaries around time off. It's interesting to analyze the result (being able to take unplugged vacations) with the successful aspects of an accounting practice that make unplugging possible.

I'm the President of EO Charleston (Entrepreneurs Organization). One of our members, Jessica, was planning a vacation, something she had not done since she started her company about 20 years ago. This is someone I'm really close to, and I said, "You need to go and take this family trip without checking in with the office." I could see she had trepidation, so I said, "Look, I'll write up the how-to for you. I'll give you the step-by-step, and I promise you'll be glad you did it."

She went on an amazing trip. She took a boat with her husband and sailed around the Caribbean with their three children. She was so glad to have disconnected from the office and reconnected with her family. The instructions we gave Jessica were the same ones we used to create our time-off module in Accounting Practice Academy™.

You, too, can use the "unplugged vacation" as a catalyst for other improvements in your firm.

This is the best way we've found to give owners of accounting practices unbelievable clarity about their companies. The funny thing is, it's counterintuitive, but getting away from your business helps you clearly see your issues. You get insights about your team, your clients, and what you like and sometimes really dislike about your firm. All of this helps make change possible.

That is why we've written this book. Many times, our clients never knew there was hope for having time away from their accounting practice and having the practice still thrive in their absence.

Our hope for you is, after reading this book, you will see the awesome possibilities for growth in your company and more enjoyment in your personal life.

Here's to many vacations to come, without checking your email!

To your success,

Chapter One
Being a Victim of Your Own Success

There are natural plateaus with every practice as it grows. It requires a breakthrough to get to that next level. When you go out and start a firm, you have to hustle. You have to take the work that comes your way. This is a pretty normal start-up experience. You go out, you find clients, and then you come back into the office and do the work. With accounting, fortunately and unfortunately, mistakes are costly. If you make an error on a tax return, it can have a pretty severe impact on the client. You need to be careful if you're doing any audit or review work.

Therefore, accuracy is highly prized in accounting. It's a detailed profession when you're starting a practice, and you're doing that highly detailed level of work. It tends to reward perfectionism. A lot of accountants are very detail-oriented or perfectionistic, which is great for producing high-quality work. The problem is you bump up against time constraints at some point. Then you decide you really don't want to be the person doing and reviewing all of the work, and so you set out to scale your firm. The problem for many is that you still have this start-up mentality, "I really need work, and I need more work because I need to generate revenue." That scarcity mindset creeps in, so you can't say "no", and this is a difficult trap to escape.

New work comes along, and you don't want to say "no" to it, even if it's not really in keeping with the type of work that you do. Accounting is a varied profession. There's tax. There's bookkeeping. There's payroll. There's review work. There are all sorts of specialties that accountants can go into, so the practice often becomes wildly unfocused. You experience heavy time constraints and lose your direction. A scattered practice is not a fun practice to own.

The "Do Anything" Mindset

Being unable to say "no" to certain work, just taking on more and more, and continuing to grow in an unfocused way, makes it nearly impossible to take any time to work on the structure of the practice. You're just continuously putting out fires.

Here's how you know you're in this mindset. You feel like you're hurrying every minute of the day. You feel like you have a never-ending to-do list. You feel overwhelmed. You're working when you're on vacation, or maybe you haven't taken a vacation in a while. You're not really taking any weekends off either.

If you feel like there are no boundaries around your time, it's probably time to put some up.

It doesn't mean you're more successful if you have fewer boundaries. What good are a few extra dollars of top-line revenue if you don't have any time to enjoy it?

Laptop + Cruise Ship = Unhappy Wife

Growing a business is actually a series of letting go. If you're going to grow your business, there has to be a natural release of things. That really feels strange when you're trying to acquire new work and new business and going from "give me more and more and more" to "less and less and less" because you're delegating work as you grow…(or you eventually reach a point where don't grow at all, and you have no personal time left.) As you scale your firm profitably, you're letting go of responsibilities that you used to have.

Virtually everyone who has successfully scaled any business knows this experience. I started brokering CPA firms in 2003. I was very much in that start-up phase. At the time, I was working long hours, and I really didn't mind it. I enjoyed the work tremendously. For me to work from 7:00 in the morning until 10:00 at night really wasn't a problem. I had no negativity towards those hours in the beginning.

Actually, my wife and I had several conversations before I started the business. We agreed that all my time was probably going to be required in that start-up phase for a year or so, and then it would need to taper off. The business grew swiftly, and we decided to take a nice family vacation. This was 2005, I believe, about two years after I had started up. Our children were fairly small. We took a cruise. We'd never been on a cruise before, so we figured we would try it out.

I took my laptop on this vacation. I would tell my wife, "I need to go check-in. I need to check my email." You didn't have WiFi all over the ship back then, so I went to the internet cafe, and I would check my email. Of course, I would tell my wife, "I'm only going to be 30 minutes or an hour." Then I'd come back three hours later. She would be upset because she was taking care of our three children the entire time I was gone. This went on about every day of the trip.

The cruise ended, and we came back to the port. We were literally walking off the ship, and she looked me right in the eye and said, "If you ever take a laptop on another vacation again, I'm throwing it in the water." I knew she meant it. That was me pre-"unplugged" when on vacation.

What It's Like Now

Fast forward to now, and I don't even take my own cell phone on vacation. I swapped my laptop for a good book. We just go. Sometimes we'll go for three weeks at a time. Next year, I'm thinking seriously about taking a longer, six-week break. I just put an email responder on and do the preparation tasks that we've mapped out. I go, and I enjoy my time off. I sleep like a king, and I completely unwind.

It takes a couple of days to stop thinking about things at work. Your brain has this momentum. It takes a little while to get into vacation mode, but once you get into that mode, I've found gears that I didn't know I had. I'm a pretty hard-charging, hard-working person, but I have discovered that I have an unexpectedly slow, easy-going capability as well.

The first step is admitting that you can take a vacation. Your business will be there when you get back. If you're not working all the time, it's okay. Your business is not going to crumble behind you.

Chapter Two
What Got You Here Won't Get You There

I think that the real danger of having those mindsets is the road <u>not</u> traveled. People keep these "work-horse" or "start-up" mindsets their entire careers. They do okay. They make a good living. You can make a good living as an owner of a CPA practice. You can work this way until you exit; until you retire, but it doesn't have to be that way. We talk with CPAs every day, and most of our clients who are selling are doing so in order to retire. It's the end of their career.

What prompted me to write *Accountant's Flight Plan* in 2010 was a dichotomy I saw. There are accountants/owners who were toiling away for years and years and years. They never seem to get out of that same mode of operation, where they're just working hard their entire career, and the whole business revolves around them.

In contrast, we have some wildly successful clients with a different mode of operation. One where the firm runs autonomously. They keep owner hours low and make sure to stay out of the minutiae of the firm. I have a client right now whose firm is one of the larger and more profitable firms we've ever encountered, and he works 5 hours a week. These types of clients have figured out that fewer total hours and less time in the weeds of the practice is what helped them to grow bigger firms.

This mindset helps them make sure they pick the right team members. It helps them make sure they pick the right clients. In the long run, the CPAs we've worked with who take time off actually become more successful in their businesses. That has been our overwhelming observation.

The Counter Intuitiveness of Letting Go

The way you start to change is to accelerate the letting go. Forget growth for a minute. Let's just say you wanted to make the same amount of money, but you want more time. The strategy is the same. You need to let go of some things. Do some real analysis of your practice, analyze where your time goes, and really reflect on one of the things that you don't like to do. Ask yourself, "Who could do that instead of me?"

Start that process of delegation, even if it's little things. Let's say you're working hard and then you go home on Sunday. You cut your grass, and you do your lawn even though it's not something you enjoy doing. Well...start there! Hire someone to do your lawn. The key is to START! As I mentioned, you can start this process with really small steps. You'll get the hang of it. There are wonderful people out there who will mow your lawn or clean your house or clean your office or whatever it is. You can start with the tiniest tasks, but start making those delegations.

Start with the Easy Stuff

Just begin to experience the art of letting go. I have a tool we call the Three-Bucket Tool for Delegation. That's available for free on our website. If you go to **www.accountingpracticeacademy.com** and then to our Resources page, you'll see it. It's free and incredibly simple yet powerfully effective.

In the tool, we have three columns. Column One is "**Things that you want to keep.**" This is the type of work that you want to keep for the foreseeable future. The next column is "**Work**

that you want to give up one day." Maybe you want to give it up because you don't like doing it, but you don't yet have anybody who can do it in your office. Then there are "**Things that you can delegate right now**." It's simple, but it's the most effective way to get perspective quickly. Just take an inventory of what you do, categorize it, and delegate. The cool thing about this tool is that you can give it to your key staff and help them re-organize their work as well.

A Story Example

This is an outlier story. We wrote a growth guide, a case study around the CPA who grew his firm from scratch to where it is now... doing over $100 million in revenues with a national footprint. That CPA's name is Rob Siegfried.

In the growth guide, Rob tells this story about how he had a mentor early in his career. The mentor didn't have a public accounting background. He was actually a former executive of General Electric.

In spite of his lack of accounting experience, this mentor shared timeless insights into managing/growing a business that Rob took and implemented into his accounting firm. Because of this guidance, Rob eventually delegated himself down to zero billable hours as a managing partner.

Most CPAs think, "Oh, gosh, zero billable hours, how can that be?" It's an extreme example, but you can literally grow yourself out of all client work and become the managing partner, overseeing the vision of your practice, protecting the practice, and managing change and team development. That's an extreme example of delegation, but it doesn't make the principles of delegation any less valid.

Now Rob's working on the fun stuff, and he enjoys working. There's nothing wrong with working hard if you enjoy it. He does the things he wants to do, needs to do, and likes to do.

I'd like you to remember you can start really small and work your way up. If you'd like to read deeply about those insights Rob's mentor shared, you can find the full story on **AccountingPracticeAcademy.com/Resources**.

Chapter Three
Steering Clear of the Five Mindset Traps

Most of these mindset traps will be self-explanatory: the "time is money" mindset trap, the technology addiction trap, the client expectation trap, the "I can't delegate" trap, and the multitasking trap.

Time is Money Trap

When I came into the profession, we had to track our time in six-minute increments. All billing was done based on time. A lot of people still do that. "Time is money" is that mindset of billable hours and equating a certain amount of time with a certain amount of money. The truth is the value that your clients experience from your services has varying levels. An hour of consulting is not the same as an hour of payroll creation or payroll completion, or payroll processing. All time is not created equal, so time does not equal money.

Technology Addiction Trap

You have the technology addiction trap. I think that is especially appropriate for what we're talking about in this book about taking a vacation without checking email. You get addicted to technology. The smartphone is probably one of the most addictive devices ever created by man. You can let go, though! It just takes a bit of practice.

Client Expectation Trap

The nice thing about setting boundaries around time is you learn how to set boundaries in general. Clients need boundaries, so your job as an owner is to manage client expectations. If you're not managing client expectations, then you're basically letting them dictate how you work.

I Can't Delegate Trap

Then we have the "I can't delegate" trap. Essentially, that's the fear of mistakes or a control mindset, and letting go of that is probably one of the toughest things for a lot of owners to come to grips with. Learning how to delegate well is the key.

Multitasking Trap

People underestimate just how powerful it is to focus. Focused attention is so much better than distracted attention. When you're not managing your time well, or not respecting clear boundaries, or not being intentional about the type of work that you're taking on as a practice, you water down your focus. It costs you.

It's tempting to take on multiple lines of work. A client will come to you and say, "Hey, you're doing my tax return. I have a friend that needs an expert witness for a divorce case. Would you be willing to do that?" Next thing you know, you're off figuring out how to be an expert witness. You do that a few times, and you have a few too many service offerings. Pretty soon, you're not doing any of those well.

A Story Example About Focus

We had a client a few years ago who started a small financial services practice alongside his CPA firm. That's pretty common.

Eventually, the financial services business got fairly large. He decided he really wanted to give up the accounting practice and just focus on financial services. The problem was - he wanted to keep a few tax clients. We had this discussion with him about the power of focus. When you have two professions to keep up with (accounting and financial services), it's very difficult to keep up with both and switch gears between specialties. By dividing his focus so much, he could see that both areas were suffering. In the end, he took the advice to <u>not</u> keep any accounting clients, so he didn't have to stay up to date with tax law changes.

After letting go of the accounting practice entirely, he was able to step fully into his financial services work. Because he let go of all the tax work, he also realized he could approach CPAs in his market, which meant a huge network of past colleagues/competitors were now profitable referral sources. None of them were threatened that he would take any of their accounting or tax work anymore, so they actually bolstered his business immensely. His financial services business grew rapidly, and he's quite happy with the decision to let go and focus on one realm of expertise.

We have a couple of examples where our clients have sold off a section of their practices.

I had a CPA who called me and wanted to sell his practice. He was a younger guy, but I could tell that he was approaching burnout. He's probably in his mid-30s, and his practice was four or five years old. It's pretty common when you reach that four or five-year point to experience growing pains. You've built your initial practice, and you shift into exiting that start-up phase.

I said, "First of all, before you go and sell your practice. I want you to go and take an unplugged vacation and think about this. Think about this decision." He said, "Okay," and took a completely unplugged vacation. No email, no nothing. Eventually, he came back with a big decision. He was going to sell all of his individual/personal tax returns that weren't associated with a business.

If it was a personal tax return that had no other work associated with it, he put it in a bundle and sold it. In the end, that bundle was only about $100,000 worth of work - but it represented a huge amount of energy, mental bandwidth, and overtime during tax season.

I talked to him around six months after he did that, and he'd already replaced all of that revenue with the type of clients that he wanted -- business clients. Not only had he collected proceeds from selling unwanted client work, but then he'd made the revenue back in six months. He was working less for the same money and now knew the power of an unplugged vacation. Moral of the story - the solution you're looking for isn't always in the work you're currently doing.

What You Can Do Now

I want you to get your calendar out and pick the time of year where you can take as long a vacation as possible. If it's two weeks, or if it's three weeks, just figure that out. Where is it on the calendar?

Chapter Four
Creating Success Benchmarks

I feel like big benchmarks naturally drive delegation. A lot of people are very data-driven, decision-makers. Personally, I like data, but I don't like a lot of data. I like a few benchmarks that I know will cause me to change my behavior. If you have an accounting practice, we suggest you track four benchmarks: Top-line Revenue, Cash-flow to Owner, Number of days off, and Number of Staff. There's a huge benefit to checking and updating these benchmarks periodically. Maybe it's monthly. Maybe it's quarterly. But the perspective is immensely beneficial because it will naturally start to influence your day-to-day decisions. If you're tracking these benchmarks or Key Performance Indicators (KPIs) and you have goals associated with each one, you can recognize what you need to do to progress toward those goals. If you have a goal of a certain number of days off for the year, you can't hit that goal without delegating. It's almost impossible to hit that goal without becoming better at delegation.

Creating Your Own Benchmarks

I think a benchmark needs to be something that you can emotionally connect with. Let's say you set a goal for six weeks off a year. Does that get you excited? Does it get you excited enough to actually commit to doing it?

For me, an emotional connection to a goal or benchmark would be, "I want to spend time with my daughter, who's getting ready to graduate." This is more powerful than, "I want to make $2 million or $100 million." You need to really break it down that granularly.

You need to get to the why. Why do I want to take six weeks off? I want to connect with my family. Why do you want to connect with your family? They're the most important people in the world to me. I want to be able to look out for my health better, so I want to be able to have an exercise routine on a consistent basis. You can't just set a goal because you think that's the right goal to set. You must set a goal that's meaningful to you.

When I'm setting benchmarks, I'm not only talking about financial benchmarks but physical benchmarks, home benchmarks, even intellectual benchmarks. Maybe you want to go get another certification. The key point here is to look for whatever is going to motivate you.

What do you really want? Why do you want it? I know, that's vague and lofty, but I think for all of us, there are usually just a few things that jump out. If you have 20 benchmarks, you're probably not going to hit any of those goals. Maybe you will hit a few of them, but you're not going to be really focused on any of them very well. If you only have three key benchmarks, they all need to have significance in terms of motivating you to actually implement and take action.

Defining Why You FTI

One of the things in our system that we take head-on is what we call FTI, **Failure To Implement**. If someone goes through our Accounting Practice Academy, they're going to have to do some reflection on what has caused them to fail in the past. Let's say you wanted to lose weight, but you didn't lose weight. Why? What happened? What, in you, got in the way? What prevented you when it came to implementing your plan. On the other hand, what about your past successes? Maybe you did lose weight. What did you do to make yourself lose weight? Did you weigh yourself every day? Did you order special food? Did you not make your own food choices? Did someone else choose that for you?

Our system is not a paint-by-numbers system. It's really about mindset and learning your own drivers and your own stumbling blocks. It's about deciding what's important for you, recognizing how to avoid your pitfalls and how to motivate yourself. Every human is different, so our system really helps you hone in on what's going to work for you.

Here's a list of some common FTIs:

- Didn't make my goal known to others
- Let my busy schedule overtake the change initiative
- Team didn't follow through without a push
- Not believing it can be done
- Can't make myself want to do it.
- Lack of partner alignment
- Lost in details; failed to keep goal top-of-mind
- Not truly "my goal"
- Unrealistic time table
- Too many goals
- Low Energy (Burnout)

It helps to sit down and come up with strategies to counter each of your FTIs. We tend to sabotage ourselves, so we have to plan for that accordingly.

How to Get Started

Again, it's best to start small. Pick up some things that you know you can accomplish. You need to get some early success. This goes back to what I was saying about letting go of the lawn care, letting go of the house cleaning, letting go of whatever it is you can let go of. Just start.

Honestly, the vacation is the catalyst for all of this "letting go" in some ways because it helps you see clearly what it is you want. You can't get clarity when work is coming at you from 1,000 different directions at 90 miles an hour. Your brain can't think that way. You can't think about the big picture when you're stuck down in the weeds.

I think a story that everybody can relate to is weight loss. If you're trying to lose weight, there's one benchmark you can't get away from, and that's whatever that weight is on the scale. That's probably the most relatable example because it's right there staring at you. It's an undeniable result of the fact that you haven't been doing on a daily basis what you need to do to lose weight. The same thing goes with your business. If you have a certain business benchmark, you know you have to do things on a daily, weekly, monthly basis to be able to accomplish that.

When it comes right down to it, whatever you can measure, you can manage.

My encouragement to you is just to start. Even if you have to start ugly, start. It doesn't have to be perfect the first time around.

Pick something and do it. If you fail, pick yourself back up. Try it again. Babies learn to walk with a lot of stumbling, going from that crawl to that walk. That's just how humans have to learn. We have to stumble a little bit.

You don't hear a baby beating themselves up saying, "You dummy, get up! Keep going. Get up and do it again, you dummy. You're such a baby; I can't believe you can't walk yet." Go easy on yourself and plan for mistakes.

Setting Up Hard Boundaries

The hard boundaries might be the most important ones. Let's say you've done the work from the previous chapter, and you've picked out when you can take a chunk of time off. The next step is to set up some strong accountability to help you follow through with your plan. Accountability with others makes a huge difference. It's much more difficult to stay accountable to only yourself. If you can, go to whoever you're traveling with, maybe it's your spouse or a child, and say, "Look, I want to take an unplugged vacation with you. To do that, I want to leave my phone and my laptop. Can you hold me to that?" That's how you set hard boundaries. You have accountability with your travel partner, and you have commitment. The "commitment" comes when you're not taking those devices that tether you to the office.

Then you're booking a trip, so you're physically taking yourself out of the office. You're committing to that expense. If you commit to a travel plan, that's a hard boundary right there because you're physically not going to be near the office.

Then, if you can cut off the devices and you have an accountability partner, honestly, you're 80% there at that point because you're going to do all the other things to make that vacation a good one.

Chapter Five
Unplugged Vacation Tactics

I want to give you some specific tactics. These are right out of Accounting Practice Academy. First of all, step one is to lose the guilt. Don't feel guilty. You need to realize what you're doing is actually going to help your business. It's actually going to refresh you. You're the most important asset of the business. By refreshing yourself, you're actually giving your business an immediate upgrade.

Second, plan ways to reduce any stress associated with vacation. If the money is the stress, maybe you can pick some all-inclusive deal or some package. Maybe you open a travel account and save money specifically for vacation. Perhaps, you don't like being over-scheduled on vacation. A lot of people feel like, "Oh, gosh, I have to get every ounce of time out of this vacation. I have to schedule all these tours. I have to do all this stuff." If you don't like that, then tell your travel companion, "I don't want to do that. I want to relax. I want to take a book and sit by the pool," or "I want to take naps after lunch," or whatever it is you want to do. That's the thing. Put some thought into what you actually want to do while you're on vacation.

About four weeks prior to taking your trip, you need to tell your key clients and staff. This is probably one of the biggest things that will set you up for success. You can't just vanish without telling anybody. You don't hide the fact that you're taking a trip from your clients. I think a lot of people feel that guilt, so they just go to sneak out the back door, figuratively. Then people are like, "Where's so and so?"

About four weeks prior, I'll give a heads-up to any clients that I'm personally working with, either when I'm on a phone conversation with them or in an email saying, "Hey, I have a vacation coming up."

Sample Email

This is an actual email that I used to send to my clients prior to a vacation.

The subject heading was "Upcoming Vacation."

Hi, I take an annual extended vacation during this time of year. This year, I'm taking my two sons, Hayden and Spencer,

*skiing. They will both be on spring break.
When we get back, my wife, Carol, and I
are heading to Costa Rica. This note is just
to give you a heads up about my time away.
I'll be away from March 19th until April
6th.*

Then I give the name,

*Stephanie Smith will look after your
account while I'm away. You can contact
Stephanie through... {insert Stephanie's
email and contact info}*

Some of the emails were further personalized.
This was something that I specifically inserted
in the email above to certain clients where we
had open items:

*As long as we can get {insert potential
road-block} before I leave, we can handle
that prior to vacation.*

This last line helps accelerate certain work that
might be coming in. When you give people a
boundary like a vacation, they respond well and
usually stop stalling. That's one of the side
effects.

It also really goes a long way in the realm of
customer service when you are taking the time

to reassure your client that there are no surprises here. There's nothing more horrifying than needing to talk to your accountant and getting a response of, "I'm not at my desk for a month," without knowing that was about to happen.

Aside from the fact that it accelerates work, it might even generate work and conversations about projects that you didn't know existed. Who knows? Maybe the extra work will end up paying for your vacation!

Note: That email was sent at the four-week mark before vacation.

One Week Before Vacation Email

Then you get a week out. Now, you get your team together. You go over what you need them to focus on while you're away. You need to give everybody enough detail, enough instruction to do what you want them to do. Guess what you're doing? Delegating. Often, there are additional delegations that are happening in these meetings, and you might come back with less on your plate overall.

This unplugged vacation is a practice run. If you have a good team, they're going to step up. If you don't have a good team, those people aren't going to show up how you need them to. It's going to be clear to you when you come back from vacation that you have a problem that you need to address.

Now, when I leave, I only give one person in the office a phone number where I can be reached. I give that person my wife's phone number. I'll say, "Look, if you absolutely have to text me or text us, I really want good news. The bad news can wait until I get back." I say that tongue-in-cheek. Basically, what I'm saying is, "Don't disturb me. Leave me alone. You don't have to give me an update. I don't want an update." The other key thing: DON'T TAKE THE PHONE. Just don't even take it.

I actually have two cell phones. We've gone from landline to cell phones in our office, so if I'm going to a business conference, I take my work cell phone in case I need to be in touch with the office. However, if I'm going on vacation, I leave the work cell phone at the office. I have a personal cell phone for maps and other things, for apps on your phone that you might want when you're on vacation. Absolutely, DO NOT take a laptop. If you do, you're just inviting trouble!

The other thing I tell my team is, "If something comes up and you think you need help, take a stab at it. Just try and see what you can do." You might be surprised at what they're actually capable of doing.

You have that bigger meeting a week prior to leaving, and then, usually a few days afterward, we do another update with them because, in that final week leading up to the day you leave, other things will pop into your mind. You'll realize, "Oh, I need to talk to so and so about this project or this client." You need to plan on having a meeting a couple of days before the vacation. Circle back with your team and go over any other details that you might have missed.

Then you change the voicemail, you put the auto-reply on your email, and you get out of Dodge. You're in vacation mode.

It's amazing, but it's going to take about three days not to think about stuff at the office. I think that's the reality, so don't plan a five-day vacation. If you do only plan a five-day vacation, you'll only get one or two days where you're not thinking about stuff, and then you're traveling back the next day. Take a long vacation. I read somewhere that eight days is the ideal minimum vacation for unwinding.

Nothing Like a Three-Week Vacation

When you can stay away from the office for three or four weeks, you get really comfortable, and you're so energized when you get back. That's what people don't realize. You're so energized. The problems that you thought were big problems at the office will suddenly become small. It's amazing the solutions you can come up with when you're fresh like that. Big problems become small problems.

A Hard Boundary Story

This is something I learned completely by mistake. I went skiing with my family on a winter ski trip. I don't remember exactly when this trip was, but it was before WiFi access was as prevalent as it is today, so it's been quite a while. In this case, I had assumed that the hotel would have WiFi. We assumed that we could go to a restaurant or a café and get WiFi.

However, where we went was this off-the-grid ski resort. I got there, laptop and phone in hand, not knowing that I wouldn't have WiFi or even a cell phone signal, which meant we couldn't even make phone calls. We certainly couldn't get any email communication. This was before I had discovered the unplugged vacation.

I was forced into an unplugged vacation for the first time, and it was the best vacation I'd ever had. Even though I hadn't done the prep work that I just laid out for you, everything worked out fine. Nothing blew up, no major catastrophes, the office was just the same when I returned, but I was very different. I connected better with my kids on that vacation than any one prior. I properly relaxed, I got perspective, I was so energized when I returned to the office, and I made up for whatever work I missed without a problem.

My Encouragement for You

It comes down to basically just doing it. Just do it! Not only is it doable, but I want to mention again that the owners of some of the best practices we've ever sold take significant amounts of time off. I truly believe those two things, success and time off, are heavily correlated.

Chapter Six
Success Stories

One of the things that inspired me to include this as an entire module of Accounting Practice Academy was a client I had in Canada. I also wrote about it in *Accountant's Flight Plan*. When we look at selling a practice, we always get financial statements. It's just part of selling the business. This guy was really successful. His profit margins were extremely high. He had a good team. He had built a great practice by looking at the numbers.

I checked in with him on the phone. He told me that he was getting ready to take a four-week trip. I said, "Really?" He said, "Yeah. We do it every year. My wife and I go somewhere really cool **every year**." I think that year, they were going to Egypt

They always pick some really cool place that they want to go to, and they just go. "Wow," I said. "How do you do that?" He swore by it. He said, "I have something to look forward to. My team steps up when I'm away." He admitted, "The first time I ever did it, when I took off in the airplane, I looked down and wondered, 'Am I going to have a business when I get back?' It's an uncomfortable feeling at first."

A lot of the steps in this book came from that client in Canada because they do it every year, and we think you should too. That conversation is what inspired me to create this process to make yearly vacations a reality for any firm owner.

Team Success Story

What's good for you is also good for your staff. In our office, we have "an unplugged vacation" policy for all of our team members as well. It's paid off in a number of surprisingly different ways.

We recently, and completely by accident, found it to be a useful recruiting tool. On my most recent vacation I put my email autoreply on like always. When I returned, I got the below email from someone we've been actively recruiting to come on board for some time:

"Hi Brannon ☺

I hope you are well and had a wonderful vacation. I am desperately in need of one myself.

You emailed me last July about looking to hire a Broker in your company. Just curious, are you still looking?

Thank you,"

I spoke with her after getting this email and the fact that I was able to take an unplugged vacation really got her thinking. She hadn't had a vacation like that in over 7 years. Her original email to me was on another matter, but she'd been feeling very overworked lately and had been talking with her husband about making a career change for this very reason.

So many employees in our hyper-connected world don't have clear boundaries around time and they need permission to go offline…especially top performers. I'm convinced that our "unplugged" policy helps to both attract new talent and has helped us retain our top people for the long haul.

Your team members will experience all of the productivity benefits previously described and it's a perk that's highly valued. We give our team the same instructions I use to prepare for time off. We also communicate with new clients, when we onboard them, that all of our team members go completely off the grid when they are out-of-office. We also let new clients know that balance is one of our core values that are published on our website. **https://poegroupadvisors.com/about/culture/**.

Busy, Busy, Busy

There is a testimonial video on our website. One of our Accounting Practice Academy members, who has been in practice for quite a while, had not taken a long trip. We were doing a follow-up. He said, "I'm taking a two-week trip, an unplugged trip after tax season this year. My wife and I are planning it out. We're just so excited about that." I could just see from his expression how much it meant to him to be able to do that. He said, "My whole career, I've been busy, busy, busy. It doesn't have to be that way."

My Encouragement to You

Get your calendar. Now that you've isolated a certain time of year, go pick some specific dates and have that conversation with whoever you're going to travel with and start making that trip a reality. Look into where you want to go, what you want to do, who you want to see.

Our family always stayed at the beach for at least a week or two growing up. Included here are my parents, my sister, and all of the "Poe" grandchildren, taken around 2002. This was the summer before we started selling CPA firms. These family traditions are priceless.

This was our first family cruise in late 2004…back when the laptop was part of our vacation. It was at the end of this trip when Carol threatened to throw it overboard.

Airport layover on the way to a family vacation – around 2005.   By then, our business was growing fast and the workload was heavy. The picture doesn't show it, but there was a Palm Pilot in my hand. (Those pre-dated the Blackberry.) I'd discovered a loop-hole to Carol's rule about taking the laptop on vacation.

The Palm Pilot - a dinosaur of a phone.

Our first visit to New York City – sans kids.
Carol posing in a Subway station.

Our two boys, Spencer and Hayden around 2012 near San Diego, California while exploring the PCH. By this time, I'd found my religion about taking Unplugged Vacations. We had a blast.

Some good friends of ours (The Kapelucks) lived in Slovenia for a year. We decided to travel with them to Italy in March of 2013. This was a trip of lifetime...took 3 straight weeks off of work... without ever checking email.

Me and the kids in London in the summer of 2017. Travel isn't cheap because it's worth it. It's cliché, but true...They really grow up fast. From left to right: Hayden, Spencer, Bailey, Brannon.

Our most recent trip, May 2021
Costa Rica.

Chapter Seven
Time Off Can Be the Catalyst

Your vacation can be a real catalyst for change. Unplugged vacations especially can be a catalyst for other changes in your practice. By taking this action and implementing this strategy, it's going to expose things about your business that you might not have discovered otherwise. It will expose problems. It gives you clarity about what you really enjoy about your business and what you don't. It removes you from your business. That helps you get a different perspective.

Also, it can help you identify the clients who are causing the biggest problems, and if clients are stirring up trouble while you're on vacation, it's probably an indicator that you need to let go of them and refill with clients you enjoy working with.

Your client problems surface when you're away, but those won't be the only thing. Employee problems will surface too. Sometimes there are employees who really step up. That becomes more apparent quickly but so do employees who don't step up. You will naturally want to give them the benefit of the doubt, but I caution you to keep an eye on employees who don't step up and take responsibility while you're on vacation. It can be reflective of something going on under the surface in your practice. Without an unplugged vacation, you can remain willfully blind to your staff's strengths and weaknesses, which means there are benefits in your business being left on the table.

The discoveries aren't all bad. Actually, they can be quite good. Personally, I go on vacation, and if I've dreaded coming back to something in particular, that's a signal. If I dread something, I know I need to fix it. During my last vacation, I dreaded checking my email. My email has always been a problem, but now, it's out of control. I'm currently developing a plan to delegate the bulk of my email inbox.

Growth Potential

Taking time off also opens up opportunities to see where you could grow and gives you clarity about what you should let go of. I think letting go is the key to growing any business, which is so counterintuitive to that start-up mentality.

It's so important that you see that this unplugged vacation really ties things together, not only in your business but in your personal life as well. At the end of the day, they're both so greatly connected. The vacation is the catalyst to improve it all.

Start Today

Now that you have taken the time to read this book, I hope I've sparked the desire for a proper unplugged vacation in your life. The incredible thing is that we've only explored some of the benefits of an unplugged vacation.

As you take your own, you'll see specific benefits that you can never predict; you'll connect with family, you'll gather great stories, build relationships with strangers, ignite new passions, reinvigorate your business and inspire your staff to do the same. The Unplugged Vacation is truly one of the most profitable implementations into your life/business that we've come across in our years of working with accountants. Let it grow your firm, and bring joy to your life. Let your team vacation this way as well. From this day forward, make all your vacations unplugged.

Chapter Eight
Here's How We Can Help You

We help accountants do a few things. We help them sell their businesses. We help them plan their exits. We help them find the right practice to acquire if they're growing. We created Accounting Practice Academy because we wanted to share all that we have learned over the years, having worked closely with CPAs. We felt like we genuinely help people grow their accounting practices and connect on a more substantial level with other accounting firm owners.

If you want to get started with us, if you're looking to buy or sell, then go to poegroupadvisors.com. There are tons of resources on the website.

However, if you're looking to level up your accounting practice, if you're looking to increase your profitability, work less, grow, transform your practice, Accounting Practice Academy [APA] is a virtual workshop that will give you the high-level strategy that will get you where you need to go. You won't transform your firm in the eight weeks that make up the workshop, but you can transform your firm over time. Ideas are like inoculations; once you've learned them, once they're in you, they become a part of you. This workshop is filled with ideas like that.

Accounting Practice Academy is all about the key concepts to help you make those transformations. Then we get you started on that road. We get you in touch with what you really want your business to be like, what you want your business to do for you. The business should be something that works for you, not the other way around. That's going to help you sell the business when it's time, and it's going to help you own a practice that's fun to own.

In APA, we group owners with others all over North America. If you take Academy, you're grouped with people outside of your existing markets, so there are no competitive concerns. We want a place where you can speak openly about your practice and about what you're trying to achieve.

We only run a few workshops a year. They have set start dates because of the community component, which is essential to implementing and accountability. There's a lot of value in the community. As an APA member, you go through three phases. The first is perspective. You want to be able to see your practice currently where it is from a high level; get that big picture. Second, we start pruning away what doesn't work and creating capacity. Then, third, we dive into how to prosper with more intention. You create that capacity, and you fill it back up with higher-value work.

Here's How to Finally Go on a Vacation Without Answering Emails!

You've done a great job growing your accounting practice. Your clients are happy, your employees are busy, and you feel like you've accomplished your dream of being a successful CPA firm owner.

Wouldn't it be nice if you could step away from your office for once and go on vacation with your family or friends without dragging your laptop with you and being chained to your email? Wouldn't it feel great to know you have systems in place that work for you instead of you working for them?

That's where we come in. We help accounting firm owners and CPAs just like you build a new vision for their practices while setting up very simple systems and processes to give them freedom from their business and still ensure their company's success.

To learn more about the ideas discussed in this book, here's what you do next:

Step 1: Download the **3 Bucket Delegation Tool** and find out what you can immediately offload to other people in your office.
www.PoeGroupAdvisors.com/buckettool

Step 2: Watch the **Test Drive Replay Video on delegation** and discover how you can free up your life and enjoy more free time away from the office
www.PoeGroupAdvisors.com/delegatevideo

Step 3: Schedule a **"Big Picture" Call** to discuss your vision of what you want your future in business to look like.
www.PoeGroupAdvisors.com/call

Here's to your next vacation, being your best vacation.

Made in the USA
Middletown, DE
30 October 2023

41601833R00033